THE FUNNIEST SAINTS QUOTES... EVER!

Also available

The Funniest Liverpool Quotes... Ever!

The Funniest Chelsea Quotes... Ever!

The Funniest West Ham Quotes... Ever!

The Funniest Spurs Quotes... Ever!

The Funniest Arsenal Quotes... Ever!

The Funniest Man City Quotes... Ever!

The Funniest Newcastle Quotes... Ever!

The Funniest United Quotes... Ever!

The Funniest Celtic Quotes... Ever!

The Funniest QPR Quotes... Ever!

The Funniest Everton Quotes... Ever!

The Funniest Rangers Quotes... Ever!

Mad All Over: The Funniest Crystal Palace Quotes... Ever!

Fergie Time: The Funniest Sir Alex Ferguson Quotes... Ever!

I Am The Normal One: The Funniest Jurgen Klopp Quotes... Ever!

I Didn't See It: The Funniest Arsene Wenger Quotes... Ever!

Zlatan Style: The Funniest Zlatan Ibrahimovic Quotes!

'Arry: The Funniest Harry Redknapp Quotes!

War of Words: The Funniest Neil Warnock Quotes!

Chuffed as a Badger: The Funniest Ian Holloway Quotes!

THE FUNNIEST SAINTS QUOTES... EVER!

by Gordon Law

Contents

Introduction..6

Managing Just Fine...9

Media Circus...19

Player Power...27

Can You Manage?...37

Boardroom Banter...45

Calling The Shots...55

Off The Pitch...63

Field of Dreams...71

Call The Manager...79

Pundit Paradise...93

Fan Fever...101

Introduction

Southampton may be nicknamed the Saints –
but they could also be known as 'the comedians'
due to the entertaining sound bites from various
players and managers.

Gordon Strachan is one of the wittiest characters
in football and his press conferences during his
time at St Mary's were box office gold.

The Scot is the king of a sarcastic quip and a
master at taking down a journalist for asking the
wrong type of question. The most memorable
was when a reporter asked him for a quick word
and Strachan responded with "velocity".

Players were not immune to his sharp tongue
either and Strachan loved to poke fun at his
misfiring striker Agustin Delgado and once
described Chris Marsden as "a grumpy old man".

Harry Redknapp also has a wicked sense of humour, often mixes up his metaphors and loves telling a funny anecdote. The cheeky chappy is also prone to go on a hilarious outburst, while at the same time worrying about getting in trouble with his wife.

Dave Jones, Ralph Hasenhuttl and Ronald Koeman have also uttered bonkers remarks in the Saints hot seat. As for the players, there have been strange musings from James Beattie, cracking one-liners from Dusan Tadic and humorous observations from Matt Le Tissier.

Many of their foot-in-mouth moments and more can be found in this unique collection of funny Southampton quotes and I hope you laugh as much reading this book as I did in compiling it.

Gordon Law

THE FUNNIEST SAINTS QUOTES... EVER!

MANAGING JUST FINE

THE FUNNIEST SAINTS QUOTES... EVER!

"To meet Sir Alex will be a proud moment. He's an incredible manager who has had a successful project for 25 years. But I'm worried about which Argentine wine I can take him. I worry he may end up disappointed."

Mauricio Pochettino is under pressure

"We'll try and win because we're not clever enough to try anything else."

Gordon Strachan ahead of Southampton's UEFA Cup tie with Steaua Bucharest

"Was that for his left foot or right foot?"

George Burley on a reported £8m bid for teenager Gareth Bale

"It's like being on the Titanic and seeing there is only one lifeboat left and we are all trying to dive into it!"

Harry Redknapp on being the team that finishes above the relegation zone

"It's maybe when you have to look when your own tree is not beautiful enough that the wood looks beautiful."

Ralph Hasenhuttl

"We're down to the bare bones."

Harry Redknapp's common phrase, citing injury problems in his squad, when looking to acquire new players

"Harry was overruled. The club did not want some nutter having a go."

Harry Redknapp on having a bodyguard for his safety against Portsmouth in 2005

"Our midfield has about one goal between them in the last year. Did you see David Prutton's effort at Everton last week? We needed air traffic clearance."

Gordon Strachan on his goal-shy team

"I said that we seem to be good people, not that we are. We can be a*sholes as well."

Mauricio Pochettino believes Southampton should change their 'nice guy' image

"If you want guarantees, you have to buy a washing machine, not in football. There are no guarantees anymore."

Ralph Hasenhuttl during his first Saints press conference

"As for wages, the players have had a trim, the chairman has had a trim and I have had a short back and sides."

Harry Redknapp on cutbacks after Saints were relegated from the top flight

"Football is about what happens in the two penalty areas. Everything else is propaganda."

Gordon Strachan on the beautiful game

"I don't know. I'll have to see where easyJet are going."

Gordon Strachan on his plans after leaving Southampton

"Why shouldn't he go down there? He's not committed a murder, has he?"

Harry Redknapp on ex-Saints boss Gordon Strachan going for the Portsmouth vacancy

Gordon Strachan: "We were boring if I'm honest with you. Totally and utterly boring."

Reporter: "What do you put that down to?"

Strachan: "Boring football."

"They have to really live like monks – they have to sleep in the kitchen and drink only water and very good other liquids and have proper food. I tell the players to send their wives to a resort and have a very good sleep. They must focus only on football."

Mark Wotte's advice to his team that's in relegation trouble

Journalist: "Have you received any death threats?"

Harry Redknapp: "Only from the wife when I didn't do the washing up!"

The manager ahead of a clash with Portsmouth

"I've got players here I can't give away."

Harry Redknapp

"Right, that's me sorted. Can of Coca-Cola, packet of crisps and three hours watching the table on Teletext."

Gordon Strachan after Southampton moved up to fourth in the Premier League

"If I said I'd go back now I'd be crucified – that's all I need."

Harry Redknapp declares himself out of the running for the Portsmouth job in 2005... before going back

"Is he trying to unsettle my entire team? I'm sick of it. It's time for Celtic to come up with money for my players or keep out of my affairs. How many more players and when does this end? The situation has gone too far and I am sick of it. I'm getting the needle."

Harry Redknapp on Celtic boss Gordon Strachan coming in for his stars

"I was laughing at [Jurgen Klopp's] explaining of my name. It's hard to pronounce I think for you. 'Huttl' means a 'small hut', yeah? So it's a small hut for a rabbit, if you want, haha."

Ralph Hasenhuttl

THE FUNNIEST SAINTS QUOTES... EVER!

MEDIA CIRCUS

"We're not doing bad. What do you expect us to be like? We were eighth in the league last year, in the cup final and we got into Europe. I don't know where you expect me to get to. Do you expect us to win the Champions League?"

Gordon Strachan is irked by a journalist's question

Interviewer: "When it's 1-0, do you always feel there is a chance of getting back in it?"

Gordon Strachan: "Yes. When it's 5-0 I always feel there's no chance of getting back in it. Thank you for stating the obvious there. That was wonderful."

"You deserve your money tonight. Actually, for having to watch that, you deserve double."

Gordon Strachan to the press after Saints' goalless draw with Leicester

Journalist: "So, Gordon, any plans for Europe this year?"

Gordon Strachan: "Aye, me and the wife quite fancy Spain in August."

Reporter: "Where will Marians Pahars fit into the team line-up?"

Gordon Strachan: "Not telling you! It's a secret."

"Will you stop playing with yourself when you are talking to me, it's rude!"

Gordon Strachan to a TV reporter nervously jangling coins in his pocket during a post-match interview

"There are about 10 cameras here!"

Ralph Hasenhuttl feels intimidated he sits down to face reporters for the first time

Journalist: "What was your impression of Leeds?"

Gordon Strachan: "I don't do impressions."

After a draw at Elland Road

"You are the agent of Lovren and Lallana? Why those kind of questions all the time?"

Ronald Koeman takes exception to a reporter who asked about ex-stars Adam Lallana and Dejan Lovren ahead of the Liverpool game

"Thank you, thank you. I am very proud about your conversation."

The reporter tries to redeem himself by paying the manager a compliment but he gets a curt response

Journalist: "Gordon, can we have a quick word please?"

Gordon Strachan: "Velocity."

Journalist: "Gordon, you must be delighted with that result."

Gordon Strachan: "Spot on. You can read me like a book."

Journalist: "Welcome to Southampton. Do you think you're the right man to turn things around?"

Gordon Strachan: "No. I was asked whether I thought I was the right man for the job and I said, 'No, I think they should have got George Graham because I'm useless'."

The Scot's first media conference as Southampton manager

Reporter: "There's no negative vibes or negative feelings here?"

Gordon Strachan: "Apart from yourself, we're all quite positive round here. I'm going to whack you over the head with a big stick. Down, negative man, down."

Gordon Strachan after a third straight Saints defeat

"That'll be the Samaritans. They usually call me this time of day."

Gordon Strachan after a phone rings during a Saints press briefing

THE FUNNIEST SAINTS QUOTES... EVER!

PLAYER POWER

THE FUNNIEST SAINTS QUOTES... EVER!

"Glenn Hoddle said I had no future at Southampton and agreed to sell me to Crystal Palace. Apart from that, we got on great."
James Beattie

"F*ck me, you can see his f*cking bone."
Shane Long reacts in horror at seeing James Ward-Prowse's injury after he is caught by Ryan Sessegnon's studs

"He's like Alan Hansen: very comfortable in front of his own goal, less comfortable in front of the opposition's."
Matt Le Tissier on Claus Lundekvam

"I remember seeing Jimmy Case clatter a player and saying, 'Why did you do that, he's done nothing wrong'. And Jimmy replied, 'Not today, but five years ago he did!'"

Neil Ruddock

"You go on about VAR this and VAR that, help the officials out. Clearly they need help. We play in the Premier League, the best league in the world, the most-watched league in the world. So give them all the help they need because clearly they cost us two points today. It's a joke."

Charlie Austin launches a rant at the match officials after a 1-1 draw against Watford

"He joined in the five-a-side on the Friday morning, and was introduced to us as a trialist. I remember at the time thinking, 'He's not very good. He's probably not going to make it'."

Matt Le Tissier twigs Ali Dia may not be the player they think he is

"He ran around the pitch like Bambi on ice. It was very, very embarrassing to watch. We were like, 'What's this geezer doing? He's hopeless'."

Matt Le Tissier on 'phoney footballer' Ali Dia's display

"He came to tell me that he was impressed and that I deserved a second chance. But then I responded, 'What do you mean, second chance? I have never had a first with you'."

Wesley Hoedt is not happy with manager Ralph Hasenhuttl

"It's unbelievable that I was subbed again and we also lost. You can see statistically that we concede or lose when I've been taken off. I don't think this shows enough respect for me."

Dusan Tadic demands respect from boss Claude Puel after being subbed in last five games

THE FUNNIEST SAINTS QUOTES... EVER!

"It's very painful... the coach just thinks that Le Saux is better than me. There is nothing else to do but to show I am better than him. That must be it as Le Saux can't do anything else as a defender."

Jelle Van Damme on Graeme Le Saux

"I'm very disappointed – I feel sh*t to be honest."

Virgil van Dijk after Saints crash out of the Europa League following a 1-1 draw

"He thought he still had it as a player and he would join in for five-a-sides and it always ended in a punch-up. Every bloody week."

Claus Lundekvam on Graeme Souness

"He was an excellent player, a great defender, but he had the personality of a tennis racket – and I told him so. And he thumped me. It was fair enough I suppose."

Mark Dennis on Saints manager Chris Nicholl after they came to blows

"He made my bad headers look good."

Iain Dowie is in awe of Matt Le Tissier

"I think he walked back into the changing rooms underneath the door, he was so low."

Kelvin Davis on Matt Paterson after the forward was sent off against Man United

THE FUNNIEST SAINTS QUOTES... EVER!

Iain Dowie: "How's the Cornflakes box?"

Terry Hurlock: "F*ck me big man, I'm down to a variety packet!"

Hurlock on keeping his savings in a Cornflakes box under his bed

"I'm going to hit you so hard you'll think you were f*cking surrounded."

Terry Hurlock to David Speedie

"Because he didn't like being called a fat b*stard, that's why."

David Speedie on why Terry Hurlock threw a pint glass at him

"We used to get in a circle, so there's two in the middle. [Strachan] was like, 'Rory. Get a few cones and a ball. Take them home, get your friends home and practice. Cos you are f*cking sh*t'."

Wayne Bridge on Rory Delap getting outclassed by the skillful Gordon Strachan in training

"We didn't get on. I couldn't warm to the man. He was very egotistical and incredibly arrogant. I think it annoyed him that people compared me to him. He probably thought I was deeply inferior."

Matt Le Tissier on boss Glenn Hoddle

THE FUNNIEST SAINTS QUOTES... EVER!

CAN YOU MANAGE?

"I've barely slept properly since I took this job on. I wake up at 3am every morning with chronic pains in my chest and my stomach. I feel like sh*t and think I'm just going to have a massive heart attack one morning and that will be it."

Harry Redknapp is enjoying the challenge at Southampton

Reporter: "Bang goes your unbeaten run. Can you take it?"

Gordon Strachan: "No, I'm just going to crumble like a wreck. I'll go home, become an alcoholic and maybe jump off a bridge."

Journalist: "Is that your best start to a season?"

Gordon Strachan: "Well, I've still got a job so it's far better than the Coventry one, that's for sure."

The Southampton boss after overseeing his first game. Strachan had departed Coventry just five games into the season

"I was thinking about the Titanic leaving from here, and I said I don't want to hit the first iceberg that's waiting for me."

Ralph Hasenhuttl when asked the first thing that popped into his head when Southampton approached him

"I have discovered that when you go to Anfield or Old Trafford, it pays not to wear a coloured shirt because everyone can see the stains as the pressure mounts. I always wear a white shirt so nobody sees you sweat."

Gordon Strachan admits he was sweating on a victory at Anfield – literally!

"I take my wife Lesley to watch midweek matches. She's in the studio audience tonight. It's one of the rare times I've taken her out somewhere she doesn't need to wear an overcoat."

Gordon Strachan going out to watch the BBC programme 'Onside'

Can You Manage?

"I never wanted to be a manager, I wanted to be a coach. But to have the power of coaching, you've got to be the manager because the manager tells you how to coach. So the only reason I'm a manager is to be a coach."
Gordon Strachan enjoys spending time on the training ground

"The kids found out first, though. I was sitting by the pool when they came running out, 'Dad, you've been sacked!' The news was all over Sky."
Nigel Pearson on finding out he had been given the boot by Saints

"In my office, I often regret the fact that players do not sit in chairs fitted with a lie detector and an ejector seat."

Gordon Strachan's Saints are sinners

"But the big risk in football is to work in football. It's like the biggest risk is to be alive, no? When you're on the motorway, you are taking a big risk."

Mauricio Pellegrino on arriving as manager

"If you don't know what's going on, start waving your arms about as if you do."

Gordon Strachan on his dug-out antics

"People don't understand a manager wanting to spend more time with his wife and family. Do I wait until people are screaming at me, my wife is going off her head and I'm a nervous wreck? I love football, but it's not an obsession."

Gordon Strachan shortly after leaving Southampton

"If any player wants to see Eileen [Drewery] or any other faith healer, I'm not averse to that, it can be arranged. I am open-minded, as I always was. My belief is as strong."

Glenn Hoddle is keen on adding the faith healer to the Saints coaching staff

THE FUNNIEST SAINTS QUOTES... EVER!

BOARDROOM BANTER

"I wasn't talking behind Stuart's back. He didn't know I was talking to Gordon."

Rupert Lowe after sacking Stuart Gray and appointing Gordon Strachan

"He and his new directors know nothing about football."

Graeme Souness hits out at Rupert Lowe after quitting as manager

"We don't want to sell [James Beattie] and we're a bigger club than Charlton, so it would not make any sense."

Rupert Lowe savages Charlton

"If anyone should be blamed for our situation it is Graeme Souness. I think he has acted out of pure selfishness."

Rupert Lowe

"We will not be pushed around by a bunch of north London yobbos."

Rupert Lowe shortly before Glenn Hoddle left for Spurs

"I liken the current situation to that of the Starship Enterprise. The shields are up and the Klingons are shooting at us and every time they land a punch they are sapping our power."

Rupert Lowe

"We want to finish as high as possible in the Premiership – and I believe it should be top spot. If we don't finish top then we want a Champions League place."

Rupert Lowe at the start of the season that saw Saints relegated

"Vision coaches are not for me. They may do some good for those with dodgy minces (eyes), but they are not for me."

Harry Redknapp on performance director Sir Clive Woodward's idea to appoint a vision coach at the club

"If we need a couple of cows to play up front for us, you are the man to see, eh?"

Gordon Strachan after Rupert Lowe said that his farmer friends felt he was a good judge of cows and bulls

"Dennis has not behaved well and the fact he has taken it with bad grace shows we made the right decision. It smacks of sour grapes."

Rupert Lowe after Dennis Wise was upset he wasn't appointed manager ahead of George Burley

"Why does the club pay £750,000 a year on someone who knows nothing about football? He doesn't bring value to the club at all. His skills are meant to be in rugby, but if you look at the Lions tour, it was diabolical considering the amount of money that was spent on it. Maybe he has lost his touch."

Leon Crouch blasts Sir Clive Woodward

"Some of his 'facts' are blatant lies. I have given him the chance to retract them but he won't front them up. He should now put up or shut up. I have never met this guy and yet these quotes have gone around the country and dragged my name back into the spotlight."

Woodward responds to Crouch

"My salary has been reported at £750,000 – I only wish it was! It is not even near half that. I want him to come out and meet me and see what I do and then make informed comment. But for him to spout off like this when he has not returned my calls and not come here is something I am not prepared to accept. It is a gutless thing to do."

Woodward continues his rant at Crouch

"It is not often that I am lost for words, but I was then."

Rupert Lowe after Harry Redknapp's departure to Portsmouth

"With hindsight some things could have been done differently, but this is not a time for recriminations."

Leon Crouch on the £112,000 Ted Bates statue that looked nothing like him and later had to be pulled down

"I remember being at The Dell one evening when we lost 2-0 to Leeds United. We had one point after 10 games, and the whole stadium was chanting, 'Rupert Lowe's a w*nker!' That's not nice."

Rupert Lowe

"Someone appears to be looking over my fence with large green eyes."

Rupert Lowe on Leeds United courting manager Gordon Strachan

"The excuse the chairman came up with is laughable. He said the club had recently received a painting of a train from Doncaster Rovers and there was nowhere else to put it!"

Lawrie McMenemy after a photo of him holding the FA Cup from the club's 1976 victory was replaced by a train in the boardroom

THE FUNNIEST SAINTS QUOTES... EVER!

CALLING THE SHOTS

"Southampton is famous for three things – the Titanic, yachting and Matt Le Tissier."

Gordon Strachan after Matt Le Tissier announces his retirement

"We reckon Carlton [Palmer] covers every blade of grass... but then you have to if your first touch is that cr*p."

Dave Jones

"There have been more sightings of the Loch Ness monster."

Gordon Strachan on Agustin Delgado, who had made four starts in three years, and was often seen back home in Ecuador

"When he was carried off at Leicester someone asked me if he was unconscious, but I didn't have a clue. He's always like that."

Gordon Strachan on Claus Lundekvam

"He will not bite anyone like Luis Suarez. But he does have fire."

Mauricio Pochettino smiles at suggestions Dani Osvaldo could join Luis Suarez in hurting England's World Cup hopes

"I've told him there is always room for bald, grumpy old men in my team."

Gordon Strachan feels Chris Marsden still has a Saints future

"[Agustin] Delgado comes alive every two years or so."

Gordon Strachan takes another swipe

"[Matt Le Tissier's] goals will keep us up. For him to do that he can't run and tackle because he's useless at that. Get the ball to him."

Alan Ball's message to the Southampton squad

"It is a strange decision, but then he is a strange person."

Gordon Strachan on Chris Marsden joining South Korean club Busan Icons

"Kenwyne did OK, he got a bit of a kick on his ankle and we didn't know if he was going to come back on. We played a bit of reggae music to him at half-time and off he went again."

Harry Redknapp on striker Kenwyne Jones' injury

"I've got more important things to think about. I've got a yoghurt to finish by today. The expiry date is today. That can be my priority rather than Agustin Delgado."

Gordon Strachan when asked about his Saints forward

"I always work with a list of five specific qualities: skills, tactics, physique, attitude, personality. I did not get any higher with my average ratings than 5.6 out of 10. And you know what brought the rating down most of all? The rating for his personality. It is only because of the fact that I could not go any lower than zero out of 10, otherwise I would have rated him well below that. It was absolutely disgusting, the foul language that boy used towards his fellow players and towards people in the crowd."

Ronald Koeman blasts foul-mouthed Manchester United star Memphis Depay

"He liked a pint and a pie."

Alan Pardew on Rickie Lambert's diet

"[Marians] Pahars has also caught every virus going except a computer virus and he is probably working on that even now."

Gordon Strachan on his player's poor fitness record

"Dejan [Lovren] had one of his testicles stepped on. It hurts, a lot!"

Mauricio Pochettino chuckles at his player's unfortunate injury

Journalist: "Do you think James Beattie deserves to be in the England squad?"

Gordon Strachan: "I don't care, I'm Scottish."

OFF THE PITCH

"We had been in a nightclub and we'd had a few words. Anyway, he came out and butted me and knocked my tooth out and we had a fight in the lift. When you are young, you do silly things, but me and Peter never got on well. He was a loner. I didn't like his attitude."

Mark Dennis on Peter Shilton

"If she's that good she can take training for the next two weeks and I can get on with my golf while she gets rid of the ghosts. Maybe she can play up front."

Gordon Strachan after a Pagan witch performed a ritual at St Mary's to lift a 'curse' which led to Saints beating Charlton

"When he sees my boobs he likes to come out with the Austin Powers line 'Machine gun jubblies – how did I miss those?' He also goes, 'I put the grrr in swingerrr. Yeah baby!'"

Actress Emily Symons on her boyfriend Matt Le Tissier

"I think there is a massive cover-up. There are also organisations in place far more powerful than governments. And we don't know the truth because we can't handle it, the truth about alien existence would frighten people. They would rather ignore it than deal with it."

James Beattie

"The odd hamburger doesn't do you any harm but you can't live on them."

Matt Le Tissier is on a health kick

"Girls have sent me suggestive pictures and said what they would like to do to me. I'm absolutely shocked by their suggestions. Then I get [my girlfriend] Sarah to act them out."

James Beattie

"I remember seeing Boy George sing for the first time and having a debate with my mates as to whether it was a boy or a girl. The fact he was called Boy George was a bit of a clue."

Matt Le Tissier

"I'm a massive Kings of Leon fan. I hope to see them in the summer. If they help us stay up I'll take a thank-you note from the lads!"

Andrew Surman credits having Sex On Fire in the dressing room for an upturn in fortunes

"Am sorry it has come to my attention I was wearing a t-shirt which has Confederate flag but I was not aware what it means."

Victor Wanyama gets himself in trouble

"Charlie Austin has a wedding dad type dance, I've seen it a few times. I can see he's having a good time!"

Nathan Redmond on the team's worst dancer

THE FUNNIEST SAINTS QUOTES... EVER!

"If there's anyone luckier than a footballer, it's a footballer's wife. She has all the money and prestige but none of the pressure."
Gordon Strachan's view on WAGs

"People will say I've got a screw loose, but perhaps I'm in the 0.1 per cent of footballers who don't give a toss about unlimited money."
Matt Le Tissier

Q: "What's the craziest request you've ever had from a fan?"
A: "A male fan once asked me for my wife's phone number and when my next away match was."
Francis Benali

"I have stuck the quotes on the fridge door just to keep [my girlfriend] Sarah on her toes."

James Beattie after news that Aussie pop star Holly Valance had taken a liking to him

"I signed an autograph and saw them looking at it afterwards. I knew what they were thinking, 'That doesn't say Phil Tufnell!'"

Matt Le Tissier gets mistaken for the cricketer

"I didn't have to buy a drink that year in Southampton. The trouble was it was the same for the players!"

Lawrie McMenemy on the FA Cup win and subsequent run of poor performances

THE FUNNIEST SAINTS QUOTES... EVER!

FIELD OF DREAMS

"I'm ready for a move from Southampton this summer, I know that I will go through some difficult moments this summer."

Morgan Schneiderlin has no shame

"I've been training for just over a month now but for the first two weeks of that I couldn't even catch flu."

Antti Niemi

"This is the icing on the jam of my career."

Danny Wallace after his transfer to Manchester United

"Four hours after playing for England against World Cup finalists West Germany in front of 68,000 at Wembley, I was attempting to clean a sheepdog's diarrhoea from a shagpile carpet at my home."

David Armstrong

"I couldn't get a club anywhere. I was training at Macclesfield without a contract and I had no money, so I had to earn some by working in a factory. It was a beetroot factory, screwing lids on jars. I don't even like beetroot."

Rickie Lambert on being released by Blackpool

"I think I was sent off 11 times in my senior career.... not counting the Reserves, the youth team and in the garden with my kids."

Francis Benali

"I've been made to look a con man, it's not true. I employed an agent when I came to England and he is the con man. He must have been calling all these clubs pretending to be George [Weah]."

Ali Dia conned into playing George Weah's cousin

"My ankle injury's been a real pain in the a*se."

David Prutton

"I told them, 'You don't respect me and you don't respect your words, you treat me like cattle'. They defended their interests and I defended mine."

Morgan Schneiderlin on his moves to leave Saints the previous summer

"I've stopped touching wood. I got splinters and was out for three games."

The injury-prone David Hirst

"I could have stayed, but would have broken my neck with all the high balls."

Anders Svensson on Southampton's style of football

"One day Saints will win the Premier League and that day I want to be back in Southampton dancing the night away."

Agustin Delgado, currently on a loan stint in Ecuador

"6 years of an amazing journey #saintsfc DESTROYED in 1 hour."

Morgan Schneiderlin blasts the club on Twitter after stars were sold in the summer

"It's like playing a PlayStation game."

Maya Yoshida on life in the Premier League

"My second ever game for Saints was against Forest and he scared the sh*t out of me."

Matt Le Tissier on Stuart Pearce

"Problems became instantly apparent when he seemed clueless of the actual rules of the game. One day, he asked one of the masseurs what 'offside' was."

Danny Higginbotham on performance director Sir Clive Woodward

"I blame the wind."

Artur Boruc after Stoke keeper Asmir Begovic scores from his 92 metre clearance

THE FUNNIEST SAINTS QUOTES... EVER!

CALL THE MANAGER

"I sent him on today having never seen him play Premiership football. But I do not have any strikers. Am I enjoying this? Do you enjoy a kick in the b*llocks?"

Graeme Souness on 'phoney footballer' Ali Dia after the 2-0 defeat

"We've had a great day. We collected a pound of bananas, three quid in loose change and we're through to the next round."

Lawrie McMenemy after a last-minute FA Cup win at Portsmouth where Danny Wallace had been pelted with bananas and coins

"When he picked the ball up, I'd be a liar if I said I thought he would score. I thought he was going to head it."

Harry Redknapp on Peter Crouch offering to take a penalty

"I tried to talk to the ref but it's easier to get an audience with the Pope. If I'm in London again and I get mugged, I hope the same amount of people turn up. There were six police officers, four stewards and a UN peace-keeping observer."

Gordon Strachan after Saints lost out to Arsenal

"The referee was bobbins. If you need that translating, it means cr*p."

Dave Jones

Journalist: "What areas did you think Middlesbrough were superior in?"

Gordon Strachan: "That big grassy one out there for a start."

The Scot ramps up the sarcasm after a Southampton loss

"Everything is sh*t because we lost."

Ronald Koeman after defeat to Man United

"[Fabien] Barthez sat in my office smoking during the second half. He comes off for ill health and puts a fag in his mouth. Is that not ironic? It's a no-smoking area too."

Gordon Strachan after the United keeper was substituted

"Van Persie obviously thought, 'Why take the p*ss out of poor old Southampton? I'll get sent off and make a game of it'... Luckily they had a stupid player on their side too."

Harry Redknapp after Arsenal's Robin van Persie joined David Prutton in receiving his marching orders

"For me it's the bad pitch and it was difficult to play in the second half."

Claude Puel blames Crystal Palace's turf for a 3-0 defeat. Same for both sides?

Reporter: "Did you speak to Jon Moss?"

Mark Hughes: "What's the point? He's probably getting his breath back."

The manager was upset with the official's performance after defeat to Everton

"Minging."

Gordon Strachan's view of Saints' 0-0 draw at Bolton

"He said that? He's got to be a masochist. How can anyone in charge of teams like ours say it's fun watching defending like that?"

Harry Redknapp after Norwich counterpart Nigel Worthington said Southampton's 4-3 win was: "A terrific game, even on the losing side I could enjoy it."

"The referee told me this was his last match before he retired and maybe he wanted to go out with a bang. I just wish he'd retired before today."

Dave Jones on the official Gerald Ashby awarding Barnsley a penalty in a 4-3 defeat

THE FUNNIEST SAINTS QUOTES... EVER!

"They've got very, very lucky today. Clearly they didn't deserve anything out of it, but that's football."

Mark Hughes pulls no punches about Everton after Saints' 1-1 draw

"When you are 4-0 up, you should never lose 7-1."

Lawrie McMenemy is distraught after a thrashing at Watford

"You could have fed me to the lions at half-time."

Stand-in manager Steve Wigley against Everton

"I stood there all day with a plastic angel in my pocket. I believe in fate – I'm as silly as a bunch of lights!"

Harry Redknapp on the lucky mascot given to him by his wife for a relegation clash at Palace

"It was the first four goals that cost us the game."

David Jones states the obvious

"You can't legislate for the goals we've conceded, they're a joke. Even if you were playing under-10s football they would be terrible."

Paul Wotton after a 3-0 defeat to Watford

"We don't want to be judged by the young, handsome players that we have. We want to be judged in the same manner, being judged by the same rigour, in the same way all other clubs are."

Mauricio Pochettino is unhappy with the referee against Everton

"[Tiredness] is an easy excuse but I won't use it. Today was not Andrew Surman's best game for us and I think he is suffering from fatigue like a lot of our players."

Mark Wotte is quite clearly using it as an excuse

"Only the first three? He didn't say anything about the fourth goal? If you lose 4-0 and you talk about the referee – it's not my way of analysing a football match."

Ronald Koeman after Arsene Wenger complained about Saints' first three goals

"I don't know how you face people after that. When you go and speak to your mates and they ask what did you contribute to the game and you say, 'I fell, I fell like a big Jessie'."

Gordon Strachan on Mario Jardel's reaction to a shove that got a Saints player sent off

"At no time did I use abusive language... The referee came over and told me I was spoiling the fourth official's afternoon by jumping up and down all the time. So I said to him, 'I've got news for you, you're spoiling mine', and that was it."

Harry Redknapp is sent to the stands after Derby scored a retaken penalty

"I don't know what Harry was supposed to have done but the fourth official came out of his cuckoo clock and reported him."

Assistant boss Dave Bassett defends his manager's sending off against the Rams

"It's nice for a bluenose to come here and win. I'm going to have a pint now and gloat."

Everton fan Dave Jones on Southampton winning at Anfield

"I wish he'd retired last week!"

Gordon Strachan on 39-year-old David Seaman's superb save in the FA Cup final

"That was not a 7-2 victory or defeat, if you like, but the morning papers will report it like it is."

Glenn Hoddle after a heavy loss to Spurs

PUNDIT PARADISE

"And now for an international soccer special: Manchester United versus Southampton."

David Coleman

"Did you see that? Just look at Rommedahl go!"

Radio Five Live's Steve Claridge forgets the listeners can't see during Southampton's clash with Charlton

"It was entertaining – like it is watching Russian roulette."

Johnny Giles on the defending at the Southampton v Norwich game

"Today I'm joined by Paul Walsh who won the cup with Spurs in 1991, Phil Thompson who won it in 1974, Paul Merson who won it in 1993 and Matt Le Tissier. What are you doing here?"

Jeff Stelling puts the boot in on Soccer Saturday

"Obafemi Martins is playing up front instead of Danny Ings... not Obafemi Martins, what is his name? Obafemi someone. Michael Obafemi, that's who! Haha! I was close! I knew there was an Obafemi in there somewhere!"

Chris Kamara confuses Michael Obafemi with ex-Newcastle striker Obafemi Martins

"Southampton have always been at the top, apart from the seasons when they weren't."

Ray Parlour

"That was a bit of a damp squib, thought they might have given us a game."

Matt Le Tissier pokes fun at Portsmouth after a comfortable 4-0 EFL Cup win

"They say an unmade bed is art. But what Zidane does, that's art."

Gordon Strachan working as a pundit at Euro 2004

"Alan McInally never broke a metatarsal in his career. Matt Le Tissier never broke sweat in his."
Jeff Stelling

"I think Southampton will finish above teams that are well below them."
Paul Merson

"Players like Theo Walcott and Gareth Bale don't come along every year, they are both one-offs."
Pundit and former Saints manager Dave Merrington

"Nethercott is literally standing in Le Tissier's pocket."

David Pleat

Rodney Marsh: "Yeeees!"

Jeff Stelling: "Is it a goal, Rodney?"

Rodney: "No, the ref's blown for half-time."

Sky Sports' Rodney Marsh on the West Brom v Southampton game, adding it was "the worst game of football I've ever seen"

"It's an end-to-end game, but I have to say it's all Southampton."

Chris Waddle

"So it means that, mathematically, Southampton have 58 points."

Peter Jones

"And Southampton have most assuredly lost their confidence in this second half."

Mike McGee

"Does he even speak English?"

Lawrie McMenemy on the appointment of Argentine Mauricio Pochettino

"Rickie Lambert's brain is very clever."

Paul Merson

FAN FEVER

THE FUNNIEST SAINTS QUOTES... EVER!

"You're just a theme park in Preston."

Southampton fans to their Blackpool counterparts

"He's got a pineapple on his head!"

Saints supporters to Charlton's Zheng Zhi

"Have you got another kit?"

Sung to Manchester United a year after Alex Ferguson blamed their grey strip for losing

"Cortese woah, Cortese woah. He comes from Italy. He f*cking hates Pompey..."

Saints fans on Nicola Cortese

"Your bird's too fit for you."

Chant aimed at Stoke's Peter Crouch, who is married to model Abbey Clancy

"Comes in used, but fairly decent condition, just no management, man-management, motivation or technical prowess."

Description of manager Steve Wigley by a supporter who listed him for sale on eBay

"Your father is your brother, your sister is your mother. You all sh*g one another, the Pompey family..."

A little ditty for Portsmouth fans

"Jose Fonte, baby. Jose Fonte, wo-oh-oh-oh!"

Sung to the tune of the Human League's Don't You Want Me Baby

"Anders, Anders Svensson, he's Southampton's Swedish football star. From the team of Elfsborg, he's as solid as a Volvo car."

A tribute to Anders Svensson, sung to The Flintstones theme

"Posh Spice is a slapper, her knickers smell of cod. And when she's sh*gging Beckham, she thinks of Ormerod!"

Saints fans get fishy

"He went for a sh*t, he went for a sh*****t.

Jason Puncheon, he went for a sh*t."

After Jason Puncheon re-emerged from the dressing room after a quick visit

"I'd rather be Bin Laden than a Skate."

Harsh on the former Al-Qaeda boss?

"We're all standing on a future block of flats."

Southampton fans at Fratton Park

"What time's your minibus?"

To the handful of Hartlepool supporters

"Head like a Wotsit, you've got a head like a Wotsit."

Aimed at MK Dons' red-headed Dean Lewington

"Lee Lee whoever you may be. You eat dogs in your own country. But it could be worse, you could be a Skate. Sh*gging your mum on a council estate."

A chant for Japan striker Tadanari Lee

Chelsea fans: "Champions League, you'll never win that."

Southampton fans: "Johnstone's Paint Trophy, you'll never win that!"

"Swing Lowe, swing Rupert Lowe. Swing him from the Itchen Bridge."

Saints fans on their chairman

"Oh Jaidi whoa, oh Jaidi whoa. He comes from Tunisia. He'll f*cking murder ya..."

Radhi Jaidi gets his own song

"They're here, they're there, they're every f*cking where. Empty seats, empty seats..."

The travelling Saints at Fratton Park

"Knowing me, knowing you, Pa-hars!"

The Saints go all Alan Partridge

Printed in Great Britain
by Amazon